I'm Tom. Every weekend I come to the harbour. I buy an ice cream and I watch the boats.

I put some money in the coin-binoculars.
Then I can see the boats very well.

The harbour is an interesting place. There are boats of all shapes and sizes. And they all do different things.

I can show you ...

Here's the ferry! Can you see the people? The ferry is taking them from that side of the harbour to this side.

Some people take the ferry to work. Some people take their bicycles on the ferry. That's clever!

What's this? It's a tugboat and it's pulling a big boat. Can you see the rope between the two boats?

The tugboat is moving slowly. The big boat is heavy, but that's OK – tugboats are very strong!

What's that?

Oh … it's a speedboat and a woman is wakeboarding!

The wake is the shape of the water behind the boat.

The woman is standing on the wakeboard and the speedboat is pulling her. She's very good!

Look! Here are some sailing boats. It's windy today in the harbour. This is good for the sailing boats. The sails catch the wind and the boats move quickly.

I'm in the sailing club at school – I love it!

What's that? A police boat is speeding towards that fishing boat!

The fishing boat is stopping. The police are speaking to the men on the boat.

That's an interesting job! The harbour police are important.

It's true – the harbour is an interesting place. But now it's time to take the ferry home.

Activities

Before You Read

1 Match the pictures of the boats to the words.

ferry tugboat speedboat
sailing boat police boat fishing boat

a

b

c

d

e

f

After You Read

1 Read and answer *Yes* (Y) or *No* (N).

1 Some people take the ferry to work.
2 Tugboats are not strong.
3 Sailing boats can move quickly.
4 Harbour police are important.
5 The harbour is not an interesting place.

2 Which is your favourite boat from the book? Draw a picture of it.

Pearson Education Limited
Edinburgh Gate, Harlow,
Essex CM20 2JE, England
and Associated Companies throughout the world.

ISBN: 978-1-4082-8827-6

This edition first published by Pearson Education Ltd 2013
3 5 7 9 10 8 6 4

Set in 19/23pt OT Fiendstar Semibold

SWTC/01

Acknowledgements
The publisher would like to thank the following for their kind permission to reproduce their photographs:
(Key: b-bottom; c-centre; l-left; r-right; t-top)

Alamy Images: Chad Ehlers 1, Oleksiy Maksymenko 8-9, 15 (a), Rick Piper Photography 12, 15 (b), Transport Picture Library / Paul Ridsdale 15 (c), Charles Stirling 5-6; Fotolia.com: Benmm 2-3, James Clarke 15 (f); **Getty Images:** Rob Elliott / Stringer 13; **PhotoDisc:** Photolink 10-11, 15 (e); **Shutterstock.com:** Max Earey 4-5, Reinhold Leitner 14, Max Lindenthaler 15 (d)
Cover images: Front: **Alamy Images:** AWPhoto

Illustrations: Mike Brownlow

For a complete list of the titles available in the Pearson English Kids Readers series, please go to www.pearsonenglishkidsreaders.com. Alternatively, write to your local Pearson Education office or to Pearson English Readers Marketing Department, Pearson Education, Edinburgh Gate, Harlow, Essex CM202JE, England.